ANIMAL TAILS

Cataloging Information

Fielding, Beth.
        Animal tails/Beth Fielding
                36 p. : col. ill. ; 20 cm.
        Includes index (p.).
        Summary: Explores the morphology and
behavior of animal tails. Includes a range of taxa,
including mammals, fish, reptiles, birds, insects,
and bacteria.

        LC: QL 950.6
        Dewey: 573.9
        ISBN-13: 978-0-9797455-8-4 (alk. paper)
        ISBN-10:   0-9797455-8-6 (alk. paper)
                Tail —Juvenile literature

Art Director: Susan McBride
Copy Editor: Catherine Ham
Research Assistance: Dawn Buley, Will Albrecht
Photo Research: Dawn Cusick

10 9 8 7 6 5 4 3 2 1

Published by EarlyLight Books, Inc.
1436 Dellwood Road
Waynesville, NC 28786

ISBN 13: 978-0-9797455-8-4

TO TJ,
whose expressive tail could
inspire a thousand books . . .

ABOVE: Cheetahs
PAGES 1 & 3: Anole lizard

ANIMAL TAILS

BETH FIELDING

EarlyLight Books

WAYNESVILLE, NORTH CAROLINA, USA

SCALY TAILS
SPRAYING TAILS

SKINNY TAILS
SWIMMING TAILS

BUSHY TAILS
BALANCING TAILS
JUMPING TAILS

TALKING TAILS
STRIPED TAILS

WARNING TAILS
STINGING TAILS

WAGGING TAILS
CURLY TAILS

ELEPHANT TAILS

How much time have you spent looking at animal tails? Have you ever noticed that some of the largest animals have small, skinny tails? The elephant, for instance, is the biggest land animal, but has a little tail compared to a small squirrel. If you don't believe it, check out the big, bushy squirrel and skunk tails on page 14.

Elephant tails are sometimes called fly-swatter tails. These tails are usually long and thin, with a thick tuft of fur at the end. Giraffes, zebras, horses, lions, and cows also have such tails. This type of tail design lets its owner hit insects that are biting their backs and legs with a whip-like smack. Having a strong, fast, fly-swatter tail is important because some insect bites can cause infection and disease.

When elephants migrate long distances to find food and water, they often hold on to each others' tails with their trunks so members of the herd stay together. Baby elephants sometimes clutch their mother's tail if they feel stressed or threatened by a predator.

CHECK IT OUT! Look how far up its back a giraffe can hit insects with its tail!

FIGHTING MALES STAND ON THEIR TAILS!

KANGAROO TAILS

Jumping around all day is harder than you think! To help them jump, kangaroos have strong leg muscles and large back feet. Their super-long tails help kangaroos balance their weight when they are jumping. When they are walking, they use their tail like another leg,

For female kangaroos, their tail also helps them balance when they have the extra weight of a joey (a baby kangaroo), in their pouch. For males, their tail helps them stay upright when they stand up on their back legs to fight other males.

Most kangaroos live in Australia. There are more than 60 species (types) of kangaroos, and they live in many habitats, from rain forests to deserts. A few species sleep in nests they make in trees, but most kangaroos sleep under trees or in caves. Kangaroos usually eat plants, and their long back legs help them reach tall branches.

WHAT'S IN A NAME? The kangaroo rat (right) is named after the kangaroo because of its long tail and large back feet, which are used for kangaroo-style jumping. The kangaroo rat lives in the Southwestern deserts of the United States. The kangaroo mouse, another two-legged jumper with a long tail, also lives in Southwestern deserts.

9

TEST IT OUT: Place a stuffed animal on your back and walk like a monkey. Pretend a predator is chasing you or that you are moving from one branch to another. How often does the stuffed animal fall off? Would it stay on better if you had a tail?

PRIMATE TAILS

Many types of primates, including monkeys and lemurs, have very long tails. Their long tails help them keep their balance so they don't fall from trees. Many primates also use their tails like an extra hand to grab or hold onto important things such Mom's tail or a food treat.

On Madagascar, an island near Africa, scientists have found a special type of lemur that hibernates in holes in trees, the way bears hibernate in caves. The lemur is called the "fat-tailed" lemur because its tail gets extra big with a layer of fat before it's time to hibernate.

The tails of ring tailed lemurs (above) are longer than their bodies! These types of lemurs often hold their tails up high when they walk through the woods together in groups. Some male lemurs put stinky oils from their wrist onto their tails and then flick their stinky tales at other males.

THIS PAGE:
Ring-tailed lemur (top)
and wooly monkeys
(right)

OPPOSITE PAGE:
Howler monkey (top)
and spider monkey (left)

11

CAT TAILS

A cat's tail tells many tales. The length and thickness of a wild cat's tail tells you a lot about how they hunt for food and where they live. Cheetahs (right), for instance, have long tails that work like a steering wheel to help the cats quickly change direction when chasing after prey.

Domestic cats and many wild cats use their tails for balance when jumping and climbing. Lion tails have the same fly-swatter design that elephants and giraffes use to shoo away biting insects.

Wild cats and domestic cats share some tail habits, too. When they are crouched down, about to strike, their tails will twitch. When they're annoyed and do not want to play, both types of cats will quickly swish their tails back and forth.

Wild cats and domestic cats also have scent glands on their tails. When they rub their tails against trees or people's legs, they are marking their territory.

TOP TO BOTTOM:
Domestic house cat (top), lynx (middle) lion (left);
cheetah (right-hand page)

THINK ABOUT IT . . .
Why do dogs and cats usually dislike each other? Do their tails start fights because they talk in different languages? Think about the cats and dogs you know, then see page 35.

SQUIRREL TAILS

What's the best way to tell someone to get out of your space? If you're a squirrel, you flip your tail up and down while chattering at the trespasser until he or she leaves. Squirrels also use their tails for balance when they climb trees and leap from branch to branch.

Tree squirrels have some of the bushiest tails in the animal kingdom. Their tail fur is longer and thinner than the fur on their bodies. When it rains, squirrels can use their long, bushy tails like an umbrella by folding it over their heads and backs, which keeps their body fur dry. When the rain stops, they shake the water out of their tail, just like you shake water off a wet umbrella or raincoat! In the winter, squirrels also use their tails as winter coats, folding them up their backs and over their ears for warmth.

BATH TIME! Like other animals, squirrels must keep their tails very clean. To groom its tail, a squirrel runs its front teeth through the fur the same way you run a comb or brush through your hair. On sunny days, squirrels also clean their fur with sun baths.

SKUNKS ALSO HAVE LONG, BUSHY TAILS, but their tails are very different from squirrel tails. Why? Skunks (right) have scent glands under their tails that squirt a smelly, musky spray when they feel threatened. Before skunks spray, they often lift their tails, stomp their feet, and back up.

CHAMELEON TAILS

Chameleons may have the most beautiful tails in the animal kingdom. Their extra-long tails — sometimes as long as the chameleons' body — are often found rolled into colorful coils, which keeps them safely out of reach of hungry predators. Many chameleons use their tails like an extra hand or foot to help them hang on to branches while they climb or hunt. This type of tail is called prehensile.

Some male chameleons use their tails to threaten each other. They roll their tails into tight coils over their backs, then unroll them super fast, like a whip.

FAR LEFT: Details of coiled panther chameleon tails

LIZARD
TAILS

A lizard's tail is an amazing tool. Tails help lizards to run faster and fight better. Lizard tails also store extra fat that can be used for quick energy when a lizard needs to escape a predator or catch food.

The most astonishing thing about a lizard's tail, though, may be that a predator can break it off and the lizard won't die. While the predator stares at the wiggling piece of broken tail, the lizard escapes!

Thin-tailed lizards have places along their tails that easily break off. When that happens, blood vessels in the tail squeeze shut so the lizard does not bleed to death. It takes a few months and sometimes a few years for the tail to grow back, but the new tail is not usually as long. Most lizards with wide tails cannot grow new tails, but they usually don't die if they lose part or all of their tail.

GUESS WHAT?

Male red-barred dragon lizards of Australia often fight each other for territories. When two males meet, they sometimes coil their tails up over their backs to threaten the other male.

TOP LEFT: Spiny-tailed lizard
RIGHT: Balkan green lizard

SNAKE TAILS

A snake's tail can tell you a lot about where a snake lives and how it catches its food. Snakes such as racers and coachwhips, use their long, thin tails to help them chase fast-moving prey.

River and sea snakes have tails that are flattened from side to side, which lets them use their tails like boat oars or paddles. The tail pushes against the water, helping them swim fast in the exact direction they want to go.

TEST IT OUT! Look at the striped milk snake to the left and point to the start of its tail. Not so easy, is it? A snake's tail begins where its rib cage ends. Snakes have very long rib cages because their bodies are so long and thin.

All vertebrate animals have a rib cage that protects important organs such as the heart. You can feel the end of your rib cage by taking a deep breath and pressing gently on your sides. If you were a snake, where would your tail start?

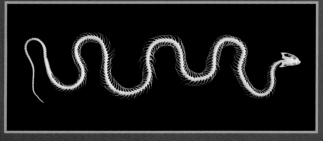

TEST IT OUT AGAIN! Now that you know how to find a snake's tail, look at the skeleton of this viper snake and point to the start of its tail. Hint: The bones coming out sideways from the spinal cord are the snake's rib bones, which form its rib cage.

BET YOU DIDN'T KNOW . . . A rattlesnake's rattle is made from keratin, just like your fingernails! Rattlesnakes shake their tails as a warning when they feel threatened. The rattling sound happens when the hollow keratin segments rub against each other.

Several other types of snakes, including the milk snake on the left page, also shake their tails when they feel threatened, even though they don't have rattles!

BIRD TAILS

A bird's tail feathers work like a rudder, helping it change direction as it flies through the air. (What?! You don't know what a rudder is? Well, a rudder is a device used for steering through water or the air. Submarines and airplanes have rudders, as do boats and helicopters.)

Birds also use their tail feathers as brakes, helping them slow down when they want to land. To reduce flying speed, birds move their tail feathers (usually 12 of them) forward and spread them out wider.

CHECK IT OUT: Find a flock of birds feeding outdoors or in a nature video and carefully study their tail feathers. What do the tail feathers look like when a bird is coming in for a landing? How do they look when a bird is making turns in the air?

SEAGULL

LEFT: WHICH END IS UP?

When ducks (left) want to feast on tasty algae or bugs under the
water's surface, they use their tails for balance when they upend.

WHALE TAILS

Whale tails are very different from fish tails, even though both types of animals use their tail fins for swimming. Whales are mammals, and their tail fins (called flukes) are flattened from top to bottom. To move through the water, whales move their tails up and down instead of side to side, the way fish do.

Biologists who study endangered species (types) of whales often use pictures of whale tails to identify individual whales. Just like fingerprints in people, every whale has different scars and marks on the under sides of their tails. Some tail marks are scars from shark attacks. Others are caused by patterns made by clusters of barnacles living on the whale's tail. A whale's tail can also be home to hundreds of small parasites called whale lice. Luckily for the whale, the lice don't live there long because small fish follow the whale and eat the lice.

GUESS WHAT? One type of whale, the Norwegian killer whale, uses its tail to slap schools of herring fish! The loud thud sound startles the fish, making them easy prey for the whale.

TEST IT OUT:
To measure the extra speed a flattened whale fin gives, ask a friend to use a stop-watch or cell phone timer to find out how fast you can swim across a pool in bare feet compared to snorkel fins. Be sure to try the test more than once.

LEFT AND RIGHT:
Humpback whales

STINGRAY TAILS

Stingrays may win the prize for the scariest tails! Like other types of fish, stingrays use their tails for locomotion, moving them back and forth to propel their bodies through the water, and to help them change direction.

Stingrays also use their tails to protect themselves from predators such as sharks and large fish. Stingray tails have one or more spines on them with sharp, serrated edges like a steak knife, called barbs. The spines have stinging cells filled with strong venom. When a predator gets too close, the stingray swings its tail very fast, like a whip, cutting and stinging its enemies. A stingray's tail can be twice as long as its body, and this long tail may help keep its body farther away from the mouths of predators!

Stingrays do not use their knife-like, venomous tails to catch prey. Instead, they eat crabs, lobsters, mussels, oysters, and shrimp that they find in the sand.

CHECK IT OUT: **Look above to see the blue barbs toward the end of this stingray's tail. There are about 200 species (types) of stingrays. The rays shown here are blue-spotted rays.**

CHECK IT OUT: Watching stingrays move through water is great fun. Many aquariums offer petting tanks so their visitors can touch and feed living stingrays. The stinging barb areas of the tails have usually been trimmed or removed to make sure no one gets hurt.

In the wild, swimming stingrays can be hard to find because when they're not hunting, stingrays often hide under sand on ocean floors, which helps to camouflage them. Divers and snorkelers are sometimes stung when they accidentally step on them.

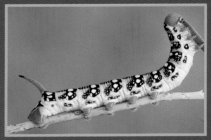

SPURGE HAWK MOTH

HORNWORM

CATERPILLAR TAILS

A caterpillar is not a vertebrate animal so it does not have a spinal cord, but many types of caterpillars still have tails. Some caterpillars, like the puss moth on the left-hand page, have two tails!

Some types of caterpillars, called the hornworms, have spike-like horns on their tails. The caterpillar to the right is a tomato hornworm.

CHECK IT OUT: Look at the caterpillars at the bottom of the left-hand page. Can you tell which end of the caterpillar is the head end and which is the tail end? Many types of caterpillars try to trick their predators (often birds and other insects) with back ends that look like front ends. From the side view, caterpillar tails can look like antennae, which are found on the head end of adult insects.

CHECK THIS OUT, TOO! Some adult butterflies also have "tails." Many biologists think these tails work the same way that caterpillar tails work, tricking predators into thinking they are biting the wrong end!

29

TAIL TALK

FISH USE THEIR TAIL FINS — THE FINS AT THE ENDS OF THEIR BODIES — TO SWIM. To move forward, fish move their tail fins to the left and the right, which pushes the water backward and moves the fish forward.

Some male fish have fancy tails they use to attract females. Many aquarium fish, such as these goldfish, are bred to have fancy tails.

OPOSSUMS can use their tails the way monkeys do, for grasping and holding. These types of tails are called prehensile. Opossums use their tails to hang on to tree branches to reach foods. When moms carry their babies on their backs, the babies use their tails to hang on.

WHY DOES A RAT'S TAIL HAVE NO HAIR? Rats cannot turn on the air conditioning or put on a winter coat when they are too hot or too cold. Instead, rats use their tails to control their body temperatures.

RATS ALSO USE THEIR TAILS for balance when they climb up high, searching for food.

A hairless tail is called a naked tail!

When rats get too hot, the blood vessels in their tails get larger and the heat escapes through their tails. When rats get too cold, the blood vessels in their tails get smaller so less of their body heat is lost through the tail.

TAIL TALK

ALLIGATORS AND CROCODILES USE THEIR TAILS TO SWIM FAST AND TO LEAP OUT OF THE WATER WHEN CHASING PREY. Alligators also use their tails as a place to store fat. If they have a lot of fat stored in their tails, they can go for a long time without eating.

MOST TURTLE TAILS ARE SHORT. Some turtle tails are so short they hide under the shells. Most turtles do not use their tails to swim.

ARMADILLOS ARE RELATED TO SLOTHS AND ANTEATERS. The bony armor plates that protect their backs are also on their tails!

TAIL TALK

SWIMMING TAIL! A beaver's tail may look like a snorkel fin, but it's so much more than that. The beaver's flattened tail works like a paddle, helping it swim. It also acts like a rudder, moving in several directions to help with steering. On land, the tail helps with balance and support during dam building.

OUCH! Scorpion tails have five segments. At the tip of the last segment is venom-filled vesicle with a sharp stinger. Although female scorpions are larger than males, the males have longer tails.

HOW ABOUT THESE TAILS? Seahorses, a type of fish, use their prehensile tails to anchor themselves in place under water so they don't drift away with the current. Males also use their tails to hang on when giving birth, and the newly born seahorses curl their tails around the first object they find.

TAIL TALK

FOX TAILS ARE DIFFERENT!
Skunks, squirrels, and foxes are all known for their bushy tails, but fox tails are unique. The fur on skunk and squirrel tails is the same length as the body fur. The fur on fox tails is longer than the body fur. In cold weather, these long-haired tails help keep the fox warm during sleep.

KNOB-TAILED GECKOS (above left) were named for the distinctive knobs on the ends of their tails. Another type of gecko, **TURNIP-TAILED GECKOS** (below left), were named for the turnip-like bulge in their tails used to store fat. Both of these geckos will wave their tails at other geckos when they're about to fight.

BLACK-TAILED DEER ARE RELATED TO WHITE-TAILED DEER. The black spots above on each side of their tails look like faces when the deer are feeding. These fake faces may confuse predators.

TAIL TALK

COMPARE AND CONTRAST:
Check out the peacock's tail on the left and the peahen's tail on the right. Did it take you more than 10 seconds to notice that the male's tail is longer and more colorful than the female's tail? A larger tail may have more eyespots, which makes a male more popular with females.

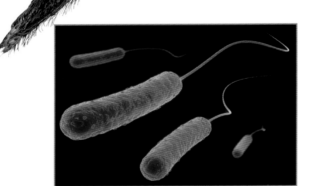

WHO SAYS ONLY ANIMALS HAVE TAILS? Many types of bacteria use tail-like growths called flagella to help them move. Some flagella are short and some are very long.

TESTING ELEPHANT TAILS:
Biologists often run tests on animal fur to learn more about them. Since an elephant's tail is one of the few places it has fur, biologists take fur from their tails to find out what foods elephants are eating.

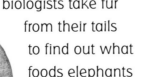

BLUE-TAILED SKINKS
are also called five-lined skinks. No one knows for sure why their tails are blue, but it may be to scare away predators. The tails of male blue-tailed skinks turn brown as they age, but female tails stay blue.

TAIL TALK

LOST IN TRANSLATION: A happy dog often wags its tail, but to a cat, a wagging tail means annoyance or concentration before an attack!

CUTE TAIL! How did the pig get such a cute tail when its close relative, the wild boar, has a long, straight tail? The pig's short, curly tail may have been bred for by humans, the same way good senses of hearing and smell were bred for in dogs. Speaking of dogs, pigs wag their tails when they're excited, the way dogs do!

Glossary

PREDATOR: An animal that hunts other animals for food.

PREHENSILE: Prehensile describes the adapted ability of a body part on an animal to grasp or hold an object, usually by wrapping the body part around the object. Common prehensile body parts are tails, tongues, and toes.

RUDDER: A device used for steering found in planes, ships, and boats. Some animals use their tails as rudders.

TAIL: The back part of an animal that extends beyond the main part of its body.

VERTEBRATES: A group of animals that have backbones. Most vertebrates have tails.

Index

ABOVE: Jumping monkey

ACKNOWLEDGMENTS

Research from the following biologists and organizations contributed many of the fascinating facts in this book: Thure E. Cerling, Iain Douglas-Hamilton, Whit Gibbons, Lee A. Miller, Malene Simon, Fernando Ugart Magnus Wahlbert, and George Wiltemyer. Australian government (Department of Foreign Affairs and Trade) Cornell University (All About Birds), Idaho Museum of Natural History, and Mote Marine Laboratory.

PHOTO CREDITS

Jacqueline Abromeit, Jeffrey Antenore, Pamela Corey, Lars Christensen, Laurent Dambies, Ivica Drusany, Five Spots, Infografick, Tischenko Irina, Eric Isselée, Anna Jurkovska, Anan Kaewkhammul, Sebastian Kaulitzki, Oleg Kozlov, Jean-Pierre Lavoie, Alberto Loyo, Christian Musat, Nature 49, Anat-Oli, Panda Paw, Zacarias Pereira da Mata, Photobar, Leigh Prather, Arnoud Quanjer, Dr. Morley Read, Leatha J. Robinson, Annette Shaff, Audrey Snider-Bell, Siam Images, Studio 37, Christophe Testi, Mogens Trolle, Ultra Shock, Tony Wear, Michael Wesemann, Worlds Wildlife Wonders, Pan Xunbin, and Joanna Zopoth-Lipiejko.